American and Dessert Cookbook

Popular Classic Recipes of the USA, from Hamburgers and Pulled Pork to Apple Pie and Cheesecake

by Jean Bellesource

"The Quokka Gourmet" Books

Table of Contents

Introduction

When it comes to food, the United States of America is a melting pot of cultures and traditions. This diversity is evident in the country's cuisine, which features flavours and dishes from all over the world. From southern comfort food to classic French-inspired dishes, there's something for everyone when it comes to American cuisine. And of course, no meal is complete without dessert! American desserts are just as varied and delicious as the rest of the country's cuisine, with everything from decadent chocolate cakes to light and fluffy angel food cake.

If you're looking for some amazing American recipes to add to your repertoire, you've come to the right place. In this book, we'll be taking a look at some of the most popular dishes in American cuisine, and providing recipes for each of them.

What is typical of American cuisine?

American cuisine has a lot to offer in culinary terms and is characterized by its ethnic diversity. There are hearty, meat-heavy classics, light Californian cuisine with fish and seafood, and lavish, sweet delicacies. American cuisine is characterized by three culinary influences: Tex-mex, soul food and Cajun cuisine. Tex-mex is a fusion of Texan and Mexican specialties, such as tacos, burritos and enchiladas. All of these delicacies are based on tortillas, the thin flatbreads made from corn or wheat. Guacamole tastes good with it. The soul food, on the other hand, comes from the African Americans and is a creative mixture of vegetables, meat, potatoes, bananas and nuts. Real classics of this trend are chicken wings and spare ribs. In the Cajun cuisine, which is French and Creole inspired, there are mainly spicy and hot stews such as jambalaya, which is served with rice.

The food culture of the Americans: vs. Europe

The eating habits of Americans differ significantly from those of Europeans. It actually starts with behaviour at the table. Knives and forks are also mandatory cutlery in the USA. But while in this country you only ever cut a piece of steak and then put it in your mouth, Americans usually first cut everything on their plate and then put the knife to one side. One hand disappears under the table and with the other the food is consumed only with a fork.

Hearty American recipes

American recipes have long since conquered the world. Real classics are juicy steaks, macaroni and cheese and burgers. Incidentally, the sloppy joe is popular in the USA, a delicious minced meat sauce wrapped between hamburger buns - especially tasty with homemade burger buns. In addition, Cole slaw and wedges and the diner menu are perfect. If you like it fresh and crisp, you can order a Caesar salad.

For breakfast, toast or bagels, topped with scrambled eggs, crispy bacon or ham, are on the menu, while colourful sandwiches taste great when you're hungry.

Sweet American Recipes

From the American bakery come lavish, high-calorie and super sweet delicacies such as the American Cheesecake that will make your heart beat faster. Classics that are also popular with us: muffins, cookies, donuts and brownies. A must for every campfire is s'mores, roasted marshmallows with chocolate between two halves of biscuits.

Americans are also big ice cream lovers. Sundaes, the typical sundae, come in many variations. Simply with cream, sauce or syrup and a cherry on top. Or pimped up with toppings such as marshmallows, peanuts, crumble or fruit. Pancakes are a sweet breakfast that is now also enjoyed with pleasure here. The typical American peanut butter jam toast is as simple as it is good.

American Recipes for Thanksgiving

The North American version of Thanksgiving is a major national holiday. It is celebrated annually on the fourth Thursday in November. At the traditional family celebration, the Americans serve up a large menu that begins with a classic corn soup as a starter. The star of the Thanksgiving meal is, of course, the turkey. Traditionally filled with corn bread, onions, eggs, celery, parsley and spices. Variants such as the honey turkey with apple and onion bread filling or a turkey with ham and pear filling are also delicious.

Everything that is in season in late autumn tastes good as a side dish. For example, beans, Brussels sprouts, glazed carrots and pumpkin come on the table. Sweet potatoes, which are served either as a marshmallow-crusted casserole or as a puree, are also popular. Cranberry or lingonberry sauce tastes good with it. As a dessert, there is apple pie, pecans pie or pumpkin pie to top it off.

American recipes for the Super Bowl evening

The Super Bowl is the number one sporting event for Americans. As a rule, the football event is celebrated on the first Sunday in February like a national holiday. Of course, also with delicious finger food such as chicken wings, pizza rolls, popcorn or sweet potato fries, which are particularly tasty with a creamy avocado dip. Typical American hot dogs provide a little more stadium feeling, for example with a corn relish, jalapenos or sauerkraut. Or you serve corn dogs. These are sausages

3

skewered and fried in corn batter. Delicious milkshakes round off the Super Bowl evening.

Sometimes it has to be quick: lunch in the USA

Americans have a strong sense of family, which also means that they place little value on lunch, after all, the children are at school and the parents are at work. That's why there is usually just a snack at lunchtime - for example from a fast-food chain or a sandwich. Some of these are already prepared at home, but there are countless variations of the filled bread units to buy practically on every street corner.

Regional features of American cuisine

With 50 states, different climate zones, an area of almost 10 million square kilometres and over 320 million inhabitants, the USA is a very large country in which, depending on the region, different culinary specialties, cuisines and cooking styles can be found. In addition, America is a country of immigration, where different cultures have met since colonization, all of which contributed to the culinary customs. So, anyone who restricts US food to fast food, burgers, sandwiches and hot dogs is truly doing it an injustice, because the great versatility of American cuisine automatically brought the history of the country with it.

Cuisine Recipes

Baked Nachos with Salsa and Cheese

Ingredients for 2 people 15 minutes

1 pack tortilla chips (crisps)
250g (8.5 Fl Oz) tomato and chili salsa
100g (3 Oz) grated, medieval strong cheese
1 stem flat leaf parsley

1. Spread the chips on ovenproof plates. Pour the salsa on top and sprinkle with cheese.

2. Bake in a preheated oven 200°C (400°F) for about 10 minutes until the cheese runs but doesn't get too hard. Wash the parsley, shake dry and cut the leaves into fine strips. Sprinkle with gratinated nachos.

American Cheeseburger

Ingredients for 4 people / 20 minutes

450g (1lb) ground beef
2 tbsp finely chopped onion
2 tbsp chili sauce
2 tsp Worcestershire sauce
2 tsp mustard
4 slices American cheese or cheddar cheese, halved diagonally
2 slices Swiss cheese, halved diagonally
4 hamburger buns, split and toasted
Optional: Lettuce leaves, sliced tomato, sliced onion, cooked bacon strips, ketchup

1. Bring a pot of water to a boil. Reduce heat to low, place hot dog in water, and cook 5 minutes or until done. Remove hot dog and set aside. Carefully place a steamer basket into the pot and steam the hot dog bun 2 minutes or until warm.

2. Place hot dog in the steamed bun. Pile on the toppings in this order: yellow mustard, sweet green pickle relish, onion, tomato wedges, pickle spear, sport peppers, and celery salt. The tomatoes should be nestled between the hot dog and the top of the bun. Place the pickle between the hot dog and the bottom of the bun. Don't even think about ketchup!

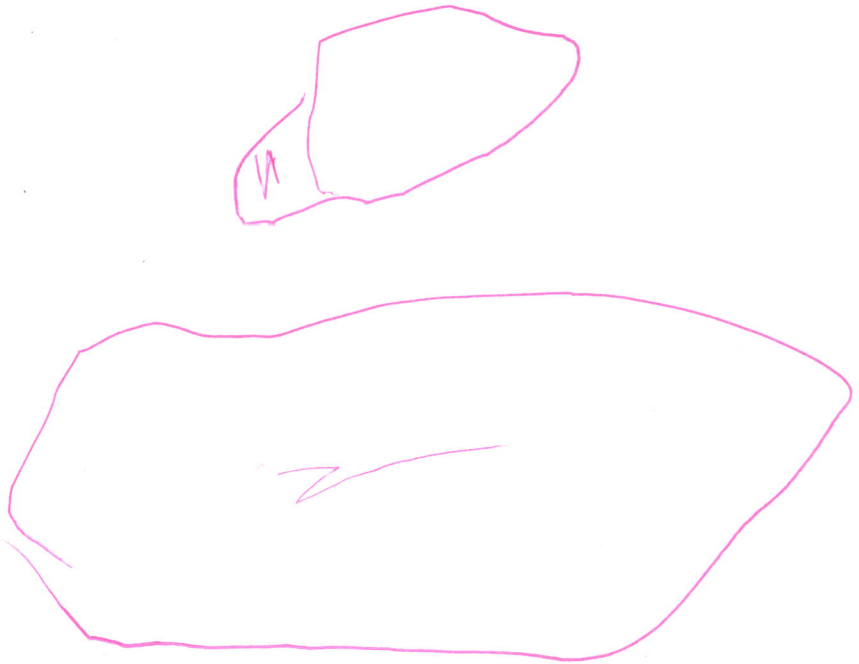

T-Bone Steak with Homemade XXL Fries

Ingredients for 4 people / 60 minutes

3 garlic cloves
1 (0.33l / 11 oz) bottle of beer
Salt and pepper
150ml (1/2 cup) oyster sauce
2 T-bone steaks (approx. 1.5 lb. /600 g each; approx. 4 cm thick)
4 very large potatoes
1 l / 1 quart oil for deep-frying
2 tbsp oil
Coarse salt
Paper towels
Aluminium foil

1. For the marinade, peel and chop the garlic. Mix with beer, 1 teaspoon pepper and oyster sauce. Pat the steaks dry, pour the marinade over them in a bowl. Cover and let stand cold for 2 hours.

2. Peel and wash the potatoes, cut into thick fries and pat dry. Heat the frying oil in a large saucepan or deep fryer to approx. 140°C (285°F). Pre-fry the potatoes in portions for approx. 2 minutes.

3. Lift out and spread out on kitchen paper.

4. Preheat the oven to 150°C (300°F). Lift the steaks out of the marinade and pat dry. Heat 1 tablespoon of oil in a pan. Fry the first steak in it for 1 minute on each side.

5. Season with salt and pepper. Take out the steak and place on a tray. Fry the second steak in the same way. Roast both steaks in the oven for 12-14 minutes for a pink steak.

6. In the meantime, heat the frying oil to 180°C (350°F). 356 °F. Fry the French fries again in portions for 2-3 minutes. Lifting out. Season all of them in a bowl with coarse salt. Serve with the steaks.

Pulled Pork

Ingredients for 8 people / 390 min (+ 480 min waiting time)

Sweet peppers, garlic powder, salt, peppercorns
2 tbsp brown sugar
2 tbsp coffee beans
2000g (4.5 lb.) pork neck (boneless)
1 freezer bag (6l)

1. The day before, for the rub, finely grind 1 teaspoon of pimento and sweet paprika, garlic powder, 1 tablespoon of salt and 1 tablespoon of peppercorns, brown sugar and coffee beans in the universal grinder.

2. Pat the neck of the pork dries with kitchen paper and rub vigorously all around with the rub.

3. Put the meat in the freezer bag, close the bag tightly. Place in the refrigerator overnight (at least 8 hours).

4. Preheat the oven the next day 150°C (300°F). Put the meat in a roaster, pour in 200ml (1 cup of water). Braise in a hot oven for about 6 hours.

5. In between, pour the meat over the meat. Switch the oven down for the last 1 1/2 hours 100°C (210°F) and finish cooking.

6. Starting at one end, tear the meat into fine fibres with two forks and mix with 6 tbsp BBQ sauce.

Caesar Salad

Ingredients for 4 people / 30 minutes

1 onion
2 garlic cloves
3 anchovy fillets
2 egg yolk
1 tsp mustard
1-2 tbsp lemon juice
Salt
Pepper
100 ml (3.4 Fl Oz) + 3 tbsp olive oil
50 ml (1.7 Fl Oz) vegetable broth
3 slices toast
2 chicken fillets (approx. 150g / ¼ lb each)
50mg (1.75 Oz) Parmesan cheese
Sugar
2 romaine lettuce hearts

1. Peel the onion and garlic and cut into fine cubes. Chop the anchovies into small pieces. Whisk the egg yolks, mustard and lemon juice together. Season with salt and pepper. Slowly mix in 3.38 Fl Oz of oil in a thin stream. Stir in onion, garlic and anchovies. Also stir in the broth slowly until a smooth sauce is formed

2. Cut the toast into cubes. Heat 2 tablespoons of oil in a pan. Roast the toast cubes in it for about 5 minutes while turning. Take out the bread, wipe out the pan

3. Wash the meat, pat dry, season with salt and pepper. Heat 1 tablespoon of oil in the pan. Fry the meat in it, turning, for about 10 minutes. Slice the parmesan. Stir half of the parmesan into the dressing. Season the dressing with salt, pepper and possibly a little sugar. Clean and wash romaine lettuce, shake dry and cut into strips

4. Cut the meat into slices. Mix the salad and dressing and distribute on plates. Arrange the croutons and meat on the salad. Sprinkle with the rest of the parmesan and serve immediately

Sweet Potato Fries with Avocado Dip

Ingredients for 4 people /30 minutes

1 ripe avocado
Salt
Pepper
Lemon juice
200g (7 Oz) whole milk yogurts
1 branch rosemary
2 tbsp sea salt flakes
1000g (2.21 lb.) sweet potatoes
1-2 tbsp potato starch
1/2l (16.9 Fl Oz) sunflower oil for deep-frying

1. Halve the avocado and remove the stone. Remove the pulp from the skin and puree. Season the avocado puree with salt, pepper and lemon juice. Mix the yogurt and avocado puree loosely and chill.

2. Wash the rosemary, shake dry and chop the needles very finely. Mix the needles and sea salt.

3. Peel the potatoes and cut into sticks (approx. 0.5 x 0.5 cm). Mix the potato sticks and starch well. Heat the oil in a flat, wide saucepan to approx. 180°C (350°F). Fry the potatoes in approx. 3 portions for approx. 5 minutes until golden brown. Remove and drain on a baking sheet lined with kitchen paper. Bake the rest of the potatoes in the same way.

4. Arrange the potatoes in bowls and sprinkle with rosemary salt. Add the avocado dip.

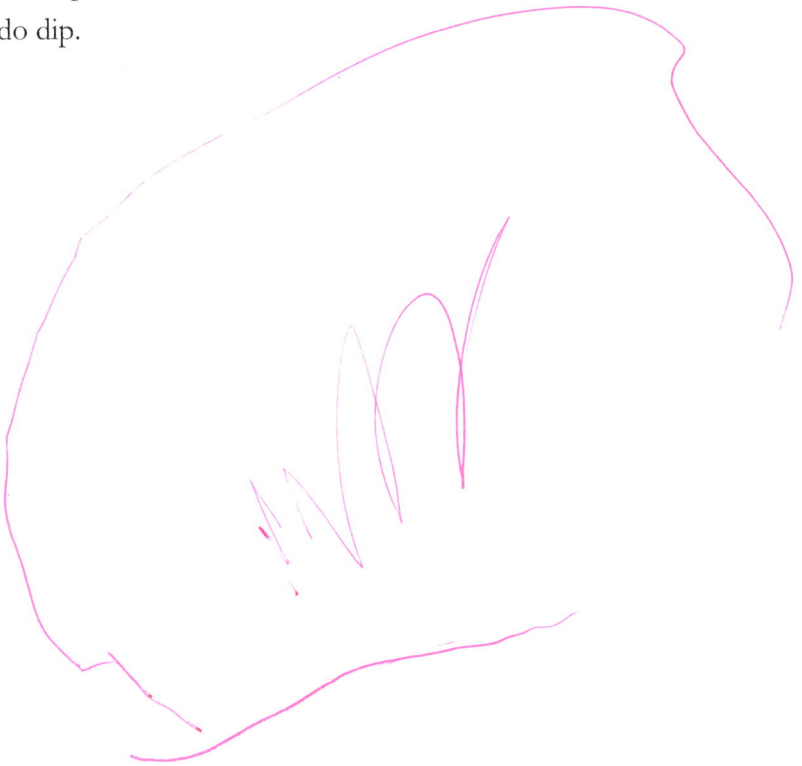

Spare Ribs with BBQ Sauce

Ingredients for 4 people / 120 minutes

1500g (3.31 lb.) spare ribs
salt
pepper
1 tsp black peppercorns
2 bay leaves
2 onions
2 garlic cloves
1 piece (approx. 20 g each) ginger
2 tbsp butter
5-6 tbsp brown sugar
100ml (3.4 Fl Oz) apple cider vinegar
8 tbsp Worcester sauce
180ml (6.17 Oz) ketchup
Parchment paper

1. To loosen the silver skin on the back of the ribs, slide a spoon handle on the second or third rib between the skin and the bone. Carefully move the spoon to the end of the ribs, loosening the skin - there should be as few cracks as possible.

2. Peel the whole silver skin off the spare ribs. To do this, dip the moistened fingers in salt, because the salt makes it easier to hold the skin.

3. In a large, wide saucepan or roaster, bring 67.62 Fl Oz of water with 2 teaspoons of salt, peppercorns and bay leaves to the boil. Cut the spare ribs into shorter pieces as desired. Wash spare ribs and add to the water. The meat should be completely covered. Simmer for 1–1 1/4 hours over medium heat.

4. For the BBQ sauce, peel the onions, garlic and ginger, dice them finely and sauté in hot butter. Scatter 5 tablespoons of sugar on top, caramelize. Deglaze with vinegar, Worcester sauce and ketchup, bring to the boil. Simmer thickly over medium heat for about 15 minutes. Season with salt, pepper and sugar.

5. Preheat the oven 180°C (350°F). Line the tray with baking paper. Lift the spare ribs out of the stock (keep the stock; see tip below), drain and place on the baking tray. Brush the top of the ribs with about half of the BBQ sauce. Fry in the hot oven for about 45 minutes, brushing with a little sauce over and over again.

6. The ribs are done when the meat can be detached from the bone with a fork or when the bones can be easily turned in the meat. The rest of the BBQ.sauce, coleslaw and bread or potato wedges also taste great.

7. Tip: do not pour away the rib broth! A little reduced, it is a great soup base and can also be frozen well!

Honey Turkey with Apple and Onion Bread Filling

Ingredients for 8 people / 240 minutes

150g (5.3 Oz) onion baguette
100g (3.5 Oz) vacuum-sealed chestnuts
3 apples
2 stem / s mug wort
7 tbsp whiskey
Salt pepper
1 ready-to-cook turkey
1 bunch Soup vegetables
4 tbsp oil
20ml (1.76 Oz) melted butter
1 tbsp Liquid honey
250 ml (8.4oz) apple juice
2 tbsp food starch
Aluminium foil

1. For the filling, cut the bread and chestnuts into large pieces. Wash apples. Core and chop 2 apples. Wash mug wort, shake dry, finely chop leaves. Mix the prepared ingredients with 2 tablespoons of whiskey and 1 teaspoon of salt. Possibly remove the innards and neck from the turkey. Wash thoroughly inside and out and pat dry. Add the filling. Press the rest of the apple into the opening.

2. Preheat the oven 180°C (350°F). Peel or clean the soup vegetables, wash and cut into large pieces. Spread on a deep dripping pan. Put the turkey on top. Brush with 3 tablespoons of oil. Cover with foil and cook in the hot oven for a total of approx. 2 1/4 hours, adding 10.14 Fl Oz of water after approx. 1 hour.

3. Remove the foil, butter the turkey. Continue cooking uncovered for approx. 45 minutes, drizzle with the resulting gravy every approx. 10 minutes. Turn up the oven temperature for glazing 220°C (425°F). Mix 2 tablespoons of whiskey, honey, 1 tablespoon of oil and 1 teaspoon of salt. Brush the turkey with it and cook for about 10 minutes until crispy.

4. Put turkey on a plate. Cover and let rest for about 15 minutes. In the meantime, for the sauce, remove the roast set from the tray with approx. 6.76 Fl Oz of hot water. Pour through a sieve into a saucepan. Add apple juice and bring to the boil. Mix the starch with 4 tablespoons of water until smooth. Stir into the boiling sauce and simmer for about 2 minutes. Season to taste with approx. 3 tablespoons of whiskey, salt and pepper. Serve the turkey with sauce. This fits z. B. cheated hash browns and red cabbage.

Fiery Chicken Wings

Ingredients for 4 people / 45 minutes

8-12 chicken wings
Salt, black pepper
1 clove of garlic
1 small red chili pepper
6-8 tbsp tomato ketchup
2 tbsp liquid honey
2 medium sized carrots
2-3 stem flat leaf parsley
400g of coleslaw
2 tbsp sour cream

1. Wash the wings and pat dry. Season with salt and pepper. Fry in the preheated oven 200°C (400°F) for 30-35 minutes

2. Peel garlic and chop finely. Wash the chili, score lengthways and remove the seeds. Chop the chili very finely. Mix both with ketchup and honey. To taste. Brush the wings with it after approx. 15 minutes and continue to fry

3. Peel, wash and roughly grate the carrots. Wash and chop parsley, except for something to garnish. Mix both with coleslaw and sour cream. To taste

4. Arrange the chicken wings and coleslaw. Garnish with the rest of the parsley. Garlic baguette and tomato salsa go well with it

5. The chicken wings are great for the grill too. Dab beforehand so that the marinade does not drip into the embers

Burritos with Steak Strips and Pimientos

Ingredients for 4 people / 45 minutes

150g (1/4lb) smoked, streaky bacon
1 onion
1 can (424ml/ 14.37 Fl Oz) kidney beans
520 ml/17.6 Oz tomatoes
7 tbsp oil
1 tbsp tomato paste
Salt
Cayenne pepper
Pepper
4 (corn wrap tortillas) wheat flatbread with corn flour
2 rump steaks (approx. 220g / 1/2lb each)
50g / 1.7 Oz cheddar cheese
200g / 7. 1 Oz sour cream
100g / 3.5 Oz Pimientos de Padron (fried hot peppers)
Aluminium foil
Parchment paper

1. Dice the bacon. Peel and dice the onion. Pour beans into a colander, rinse with cold water. Drain. Wash and roughly dice tomatoes. Leave the bacon in a saucepan, remove it. Add 2 tablespoons of oil, sauté the onions until translucent.

2. Add tomato paste, sweat. Add the tomatoes, beans and the rendered bacon, bring to the boil and stew for 8–10 minutes. Season well with salt, cayenne pepper and pepper. Then mash lightly with a fork.

3. Wrap flat cakes stacked in aluminium foil. Place on half of a parchment-lined baking sheet. Heat in a preheated oven 180°C (350°F) for 10–15 minutes.

4. Heat 2 tablespoons of oil in a pan, sear the meat on each side over high heat. Season with salt and pepper, place on the free side of the baking sheet and bake at the same temperature for the remaining 5–6 minutes.

5. Coarsely grate the cheese. Stir the sour cream until smooth, season with salt and pepper. Wash the peppers and pat dry. Heat 3 tablespoons of oil in a small pan, add the peppers and fry briefly. Remove and sprinkle with coarse salt.

6. Take the meat out of the oven. Let rest for 1 minute, cut into slices.

7. Arrange flatbreads with bean and tomato puree, steak strips, sour cream, chili peppers and cheese.

Blackened Red Snapper

Ingredients for 4 people / 40 minutes

2 small onions
3 tbsp White wine vinegar
Salt, pepper, sugar
9 tbsp olive oil
1 small romaine lettuce
100g (1/4lb) cherry tomatoes
2-3 stem basil
1 clove of garlic
1 tsp dried thyme
1 tbsp sweet paprika
1 tsp cayenne and
Lemon pepper, 5 tbsp butter
800g (2lb) red snapper fillet (fresh or frozen; alternatively, cod or ling fish fillet)
1 ripe avocado
Grapefruit

1. Peel the onions and finely dice them. Mix half with vinegar, salt, pepper and a pinch of sugar. Beat in 3 tablespoons of oil. Clean and wash the lettuce and pluck it smaller. Wash tomatoes and cut in half

2. Wash and finely chop the basil. Peel and chop the garlic. Mix the onion, thyme, paprika, 1 teaspoon salt, cayenne and lemon pepper in a deep plate with the rest. Melt the butter and mix with 6 tablespoons of oil in a deep plate

3. Wash the fish, pat dry and cut into 8 pieces. Turn first in the fat and then in the seasoning mixture. Fry in a hot pan without additional fat for 3-4 minutes on each side

4. Halve, stone, peel and slice the avocado. Mix with lettuce, tomatoes and dressing. Arrange everything. Garnish with grapefruit and basil. French fries, ketchup and mayonnaise go well with it. Drink: cool white wine

Grilled Quesadillas with Guacamole

Ingredients for 6 people / 45 minutes

6 rump steaks (approx. 120g / ¼ lb. each)
salt
pepper
3 red onions
1 large bunch of spring onions
320g (10.77 Fl Oz) can of vegetable corn
320g (10.77 Fl Oz can) of kidney beans
250g (8.4 Oz) cheddar cheese
2 large avocados
1 shallot
3 garlic cloves
1 chili pepper
Juice of 1/2 lime
6 tortilla cake
6 tbsp Sour cream

1. Season the rump steaks with salt and pepper and grill them on the grill for approx. 3 minutes on both sides or with a core temperature of 54°C (129°F) medium rare. Let the steaks cool and cut into strips

2. Peel the onions and cut into strips. Wash the spring onions, shake dry, clean and cut into fine rings. Drain the corn and kidney beans. Coarsely grate the cheese

3. Halve the avocados, remove the seeds, remove the pulp from the skin with a spoon and place in a bowl. Crush the pulp to a pulp with a fork. Peel and finely chop shallot and garlic. Wash the chili pepper, remove the core and cut into fine strips. Mix the shallot, garlic and chili with the avocado, season with lime juice, salt and pepper

4. Cover half of each tortilla flat with 1/6 of the rump steak strips, onions, spring onions, corn, kidney beans and grated cheese. Fold up and grill on both sides on the grill until golden brown until the cheese has melted

5. Halve tortilla cakes, serve with guacamole and sour cream

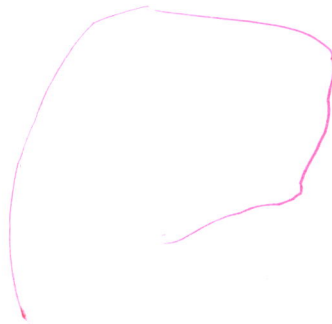

American Coleslaw

Ingredients for 6 people / 30 minutes

1 white cabbage (approx. 1.4 kg / 3lb)
2 big carrots
1 onion
150g (5.3 Oz) solid sour cream
6 tbsp mayonnaise
3-4 tbsp white wine vinegar
salt and pepper
sugar

1. Remove the outer leaves from the cabbage and discard. Wash the cabbage and cut into quarters. Cut out the stalk in a wedge shape.

2. Halve the cabbage quarter lengthways and slice or slice into very fine strips on a kitchen slicer or with a knife. Transfer to a large bowl.

3. Clean, peel and roughly grate the carrots into the cabbage. Peel and dice the onion. Mix and knead everything with your hands. This will make the cabbage softer.

4. For the sauce, mix together sour cream, mayonnaise, vinegar, 2 teaspoons of salt, 1 teaspoon of pepper and 1 teaspoon of sugar. Mix the coleslaw and sauce well with your hands. Cover the Cole Slaw and chill for at least 4 hours.

5. Then season to taste again with salt, pepper and vinegar. Tastes great with veal knuckle, steak, burger or spare ribs.

6. Cole Slaw with Raisins & Nuts: Wash 50g (1.76oz) raisins and pat dry. Roughly chop 50g (1.76oz) of hazelnuts. Raise both under the Cole Slaw.

Chicken Club Sandwich

Ingredients for 4 people / 45 min / Waiting time 20 min

1 clove of garlic
4 tbsp olive oil
2 tbsp Worcestershire Sauce
Salt
Pepper
Rose peppers
400g (1lb) chicken fillet
1 ripe avocado
1-2 tbsp lemon juice
Cumin
Green pepper sauce
8 slices breakfast bacon
8 sheets lettuce
1 Beefsteak tomato
1 onion
1/2 bunch coriander
8 slices whole wheat sandwich toast

1. Peel the garlic and press it through a garlic press. Mix together the oil and Worcestershire sauce and season with salt, pepper, garlic and paprika.

2. Wash the meat, pat dry and turn in the marinade. Chill for about 30 minutes.

3. In the meantime, halve the avocado, remove the stone, remove the pulp from the skin with a spoon and puree. Season savoury with salt, lemon juice, cumin and pepper sauce.

4. Remove the chicken fillet from the marinade and stir-fry in a hot pan for about 6 minutes. Take out meat. Fry the bacon in it until crispy.

5. Wash the lettuce and shake dry. Wash and clean the tomato and cut into thin slices. Peel the onion and cut into rings. Wash the coriander and shake dry.

6. Cut the meat n thin slices. Toast bread and brush with avocado cream.

7. Cover 4 slices one after the other with 1 lettuce leaf, meat, 2 tomato slices, onion, coriander, bacon and lettuce each. Finish with the second slice of bread and cut sandwiches in half

Dessert Recipes

Classic American Cheesecake

Ingredients for 12 pieces / Preparation 90 minutes

125g (4.41 Oz) butter
250g (8.81 Oz) crispy whole oat biscuits
900g (31.74 Oz) room warm double cream cheese
300g (10.58 Oz) sugar
food starch
1 tsp vanilla extract
1 Egg
180ml (6.17 Oz) whipped cream
Fat and flour
Large freezer bag
Aluminium foil
Cling film

1. Melt butter in a saucepan for the bottom. Remove from the stove and let cool down a bit. Put the biscuits in a large freezer bag and crumble them finely with a rolling pin. Mix the biscuit crumbs and butter well.

2. Grease the springform pan (26 cm Ø) and sprinkle with flour. Put the crumbs in the springform pan, press firmly to form a smooth base. Chill for about 30 minutes.

3. Place two strips of aluminium foil (approx. 38 cm each) crosswise on the work surface, place the springform pan in the middle. Fold the foil up and down on the outer wall of the springform pan, press down tightly.

4. Mix the cream cheese, sugar, starch and vanilla extract together. Mix in eggs and cream one after the other. Pour the cheese cream on the bottom. Place the dish on the drip pan of the oven and pour enough hot water into the drip pan so that the water reaches the edge of the springform pan approx. 2.5 cm.

5. Bake in a preheated oven 180°C (350°F) for about 1 hour until the cream hardly wobbles when you gently shake the pan.

6. Take out of the oven, remove the foil. Let the cake cool in the tin on a wire rack for about 1 hour. Cover with cling film and put in the refrigerator for at least 4.5 hours, or preferably overnight

7. Then remove the cake from the mould, arrange and cut into pieces.

American Apple Pie (covered apple pie)

Ingredients for 12 pieces / 60 minutes

210g (7.05 Oz) cold butter
100g (3.52 Oz) cold clarified butter / lard
400g (14.10 Oz) flour
2 tbsp sugar
Salt
Flour
Fat and flour
Cling film
100g (3.31 lb.) sour apples
1 tsp cinnamon
3 tbsp lemon juice
2 tbsp maple syrup
3 tbsp flour
5 tbsp ground almonds (skinless)
1-2 tsp sugar

1. For the dough, cut the butter and lard into small pieces and freeze for about 30 minutes. Mix flour, 2 tablespoons sugar and 1 teaspoon (3 g) salt. Add the butter, lard and 150ml (5.07 Fl Oz) ice-cold water to the flour mixture.

2. First mix everything with the dough hook of the mixer. Then knead briefly with your hands until you have a smooth dough. Shape into a ball on a little flour. Wrap in foil and put in the fridge for about 2 hours.

3. Grease a pie or tart pan with a base that can be lifted out (26 cm Ø; 4 cm high) and dust with flour.

4. For the filling, peel, quarter and core the apples. Halve the apple quarters lengthways and cut across into thin slices. Mix with cinnamon, lemon juice, maple syrup, 3 tablespoons flour and 3 tablespoons almonds. Roll out half of the dough in a round shape (approx. 30 cm Ø) on a little flour.

5. Line the mould with it and press the dough onto the edge.

6. Sprinkle the pastry base with 2 tbsp almonds. Spread the apple mixture on top in a light dome shape. Brush the edge of the pastry with 1 tbsp maple syrup. Roll out the rest of the dough in a round shape (approx. 27 cm Ø) on a little flour and place on the cake.

7. Cut off the excess edge, press the dough together at the edge with your fingers. Cut a star shape in the middle of the dough lid. Brush the pastry lid with 1 tbsp maple syrup. In the preheated oven 200°C (400°F) for approx. 45 minutes (possibly cover after approx. 40 minutes). Sprinkle with 1-2 teaspoons of sugar and serve warm.

Nut Tart

Ingredients for 12 pieces / 75 minutes / Waiting time 30 minutes

210g (7.o5 Oz) flour
280g (9.7 Oz) cold butter
1/4 tsp salt
100g (3.53 Oz) sugar
1 packet vanillin sugar
4 eggs
180ml (6.17 Oz) beet syrup
260g (8.81 Oz) pecan kernels
Flour
Fat
Cling film
Parchment paper

1. Knead the flour, 2/3 of the butter, 3 tablespoons water and salt to form a smooth dough. Wrap the dough in cling film and refrigerate for about 30 minutes.

2. Roll out the dough round on baking paper (approx. 30 cm Ø) and place in the greased tart pan (26 cm Ø), remove the baking paper. Press the dough onto the edge. Fold excess dough inwards and press on. Prick the bottom several times with a fork.

3. Beat the rest of the soft butter, sugar and vanilla sugar with the whisk of the hand mixer for about 5 minutes until creamy. Stir in eggs one at a time. Fold in the beet syrup. Fold ¾ of nuts into the mixture and pour into the mould. Scatter the remaining nuts on the tart.

4. Bake the tart in the preheated oven 160°C (325°F) on the lower rack for about 45 minutes. (If the filling gets too dark, lower the heat)

Key Lime Pie

Ingredients For 12 pieces / 50 minutes

100g (3.53 Oz) coconut oil
200g (7.05 Oz) white couverture
100g (3.52 Oz) cornflakes
100g (3.52 Oz) ladyfingers
3-4 organic lemons
4 eggs
1 can (410ml / 14.10 Oz) sweetened condensed milk, heat-treated
50ml 1.7 Oz whipped cream
15g / o.53 Oz butter
360g (12. 3 Oz) sugar
70g (2.3 Oz) food starch
2 Egg yolk
Oil
2 freeze bags

1. Brush a tart pan with a lift-off base (26 cm Ø) with oil. Melt coconut oil and chocolate in a saucepan while stirring. Place the cornflakes and ladyfingers in a freezer bag and crush them finely with a rolling pin. Mix the crumbs well with the chocolate and press them evenly into the mould to form the base and edge. Chill the mould for at least 1 hour

2. Wash 2 lemons thoroughly, pat dry and finely rub the peel. Squeeze all the lemons and measure out 5.07 FL Oz of juice. Set aside 1 tablespoon of lemon juice. Separate the eggs and refrigerate the egg whites. Bring the condensed milk, cream, butter, 3.52 Oz sugar, 8.45 FL Oz water and the lemon peel to the boil in a saucepan while stirring. Mix 5.07 FL Oz lemon juice and corn-starch. Take the saucepan off the heat, stir in the corn-starch and place back on the hot stove.

3. Bring to the boil while stirring and simmer for about 1 minute. Whisk 6 egg yolks. Stir 1–2 tablespoons of hot cream into the egg yolks, then stir the egg yolk mixture into the hot cream. Carefully distribute the cream on the chilled crumble base and smooth it out. Let cool for about 30 minutes, then chill for about 2 hours

4. Beat the egg whites until stiff, pour in 8.81 Oz of sugar and continue beating until the sugar has dissolved. Finally add 1 tablespoon of lemon juice and whisk in. Spread the meringue mass in a wavy manner on the cream and lightly brown with a kitchen gas burner. If possible, eat the pie on the same day

5. Waiting time approx. 3 1/2 hours

Pumpkin Pie

Ingredients for 12 pieces / 120 min (+ 180 min waiting time)

210g (7.05 Oz) flour
1 tsp baking powder
260g (8.8 Oz) sugar
Salt
3 eggs
100g (3.5 Oz) butter
1 Hokkaido pumpkin (800g / 2lb)
200ml (6.76 Fl Oz) milk
60g 2.11 Oz brown sugar
1 1/2 tsp ground cinnamon
1/2 tsp ground ginger
1 pinch ground nutmeg
1/2 pinch ground clove
Flour
Fat
Cling film
Parchment paper
Dry peas

1. Mix the flour, baking powder, 3.5 Oz sugar and a pinch of salt in a bowl. Add 1 egg, butter in pieces and possibly 1 tablespoon of cold water and knead everything into a smooth short crust pastry. Wrap in foil and refrigerate for about 30 minutes.

2. In the meantime, clean the pumpkin and cut the pumpkin meat (approx. 17.63 Oz net) into cubes. Put in a saucepan, cover with water, bring to the boil and cook covered over medium heat for 10-12 minutes. Let the remaining water drain well. Finely puree the pumpkin with a cutting stick. Separate the remaining eggs. Add the milk, remaining sugar, egg yolk, a pinch of salt, cinnamon, ginger, nutmeg and clove, mix well and allow to cool.

3. Roll out the short crust pastry on a floured work surface in a round shape (approx. 32 cm Ø). Line a greased pie tin (approx. 26 cm Ø) dusted with flour with it and cut off any excess dough. Prick the pastry base several times with a fork and cover with baking paper. Fill in peas for blind baking and bake in the preheated oven 200°C (400°F) for 15-20 minutes. Take the peas and baking paper out of the mould and bake the base for another 5 minutes.

4. Beat the egg whites with the whisk of the hand mixer until stiff and stir carefully into the cold pumpkin puree. Spread the pumpkin mixture on the pre-baked base. Bake the pie in the preheated oven 160°C (325°F) for 45–50 minutes. Let cool on a wire rack. Whipped cream tastes good with it.

Classic Blueberry Muffins

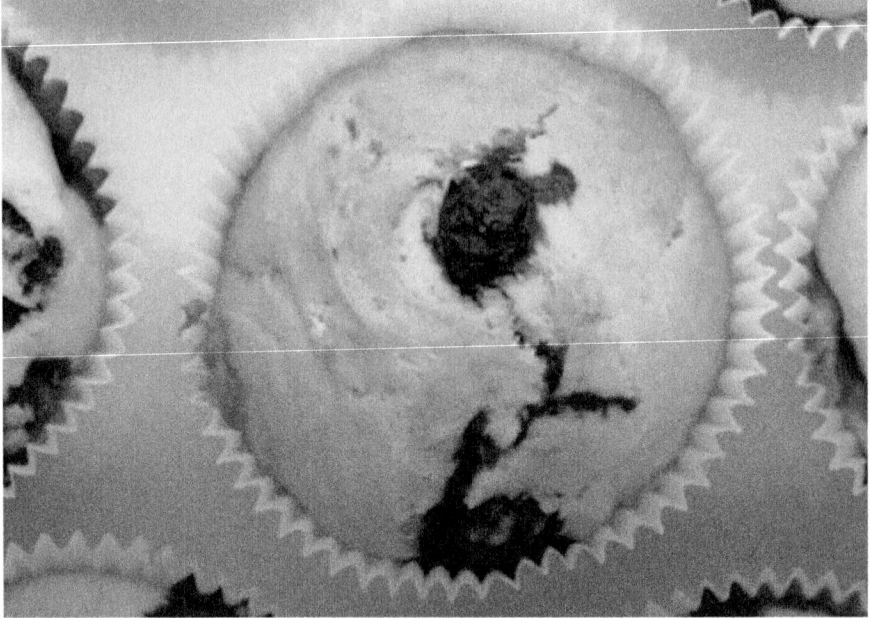

Ingredients for 12 pieces / Preparation 40 minutes

250g (8.8 Oz) blueberries fresh or frozen
125g (4.41 Oz) butter
135g (4.76 Oz) sugar
1/2 tsp vanilla sugar
2 eggs
120ml (4.22 Fl Oz) milk
360g (12.35 Oz) Flour
2 tsp baking powder
1/4 tsp salt

1. Wash fresh blueberries and drain well. Thaw frozen blueberries and then drain well without breaking them. Line a 12-cup muffin pan with paper liners.

2. Melt butter. Use the whisk to stir the sugar and vanilla sugar into the hot butter, then stir in the eggs and milk.

3. Mix the flour with baking powder and salt and add to the liquid ingredients. Mix very lightly and carefully fold in the blueberries. Tip for thawed berries: dust with flour, mix carefully and only then fold in.

4. Spread the batter evenly on the muffin tin. Bake the muffins in the preheated oven 190°C (375°F) for about 18 minutes and make a cooking test. To do this, prick into a muffin with a wooden skewer. If the skewer stays clean, the muffins are ready. If there is still some batter stuck to it, return to the oven and bake for a few minutes longer.

Oreo Cheesecake Cookies

Ingredients for 24 pieces / 60 minutes

12 Chocolate biscuits with cream filling
125ml (4.23 Oz) soft butter
180g (6.17 Oz) sugar
125g (4.23 Oz) room warm double cream cheese
180g (6.172 Oz) flour
1/2 tsp baking powder
Parchment paper

1. Chop the biscuits into small pieces. Beat the butter and sugar with the whisk of the hand mixer until creamy. Add the cream cheese and continue beating. Mix the flour and baking powder and stir in. Carefully stir the biscuits into the batter, except for a tablespoon. Chill for about 1 hour.

2. Line 2 baking sheets with parchment paper. Cut the dough in half and form 24–26 balls of the same size. Spread on the baking sheets, leaving enough space. Press the balls slightly flat, distribute the remaining biscuit crumbs on top and press down lightly.

3. Bake trays one after the other in the preheated oven 180°C (350°F) for approx. 14 minutes. Take out of the oven and let cool down on a wire rack.

Decorated Donuts

Ingredients for 30 pieces / 90 min

250g (8.81 Oz) flour
10g (0.4 Oz) fresh yeast
1 tbsp +100g (3.35 Oz) sugar
125ml (4.22 Fl Oz) milk
1 Organic lemon
50g (1.76 Oz) butter or margarine
1 egg
1l / 1 quart vegetable oil for deep-frying
150g (5.29 Oz) dark chocolate couverture
30g (1.05 Oz) white couverture
50g (1.7 Oz) powdered sugar
1 tbsp pink sugar sprinkles
1-2 tbsp gold-white sugar pearls
Flour
1 disposable piping bags

1. Put the flour in a bowl, make a well in the middle, crumble the yeast into it. Add 1 tablespoon of sugar. Warm the milk, pour approx. 1/3 of the yeast into the well and mix with a little flour from the edge to form a pre-dough. Cover and let rise in a warm place for about 10 minutes.

2. Wash the lemon thoroughly, pat dry, finely grate the peel. Dice the fat. Add egg, fat, rest of milk, half of the sugar and lemon zest to the pre-dough. Knead well with the dough hook of the hand mixer for 3–4 minutes. Cover and let rise in a warm place for about 30 minutes.

3. Place the dough on a well-floured work surface, knead again briefly and roll out approx. 1 cm thick. Cut out donuts with a donut cutter (approx. 5 cm Ø). Place on a floured baking sheet.

4. Knead, roll out and cut out the leftover dough again and again until the dough is used up. Cover the donuts and let rise for 5–10 minutes.

5. Heat the oil in a high saucepan to 150°C (300°F). Carefully pour the donuts into the hot oil in portions and bake for 1–2 minutes while turning until golden brown. Lift out with a slotted spoon, drain on kitchen paper and allow to cool.

6. Turn some donuts in the remaining sugar while they are still hot and allow to cool.

7. Roughly chop the couverture and melt separately over a warm water bath. Squeeze 1/2 lemon. Mix powdered sugar and approx. 1 tbsp lemon juice to form a smooth, thick glaze. Garnish some donuts with icing and pink sugar sprinkles.

8. Dip the rest in dark couverture, decorate with white couverture or sprinkle with gold and white sugar pearls. Let dry.

Chocolate Lover's Peanut Brownie

Ingredients for 25 pieces / 50 min

250g (8.81 Oz) butter + something to grease
200g (7.05 Oz) flour + something to dust
300g (10.6 Oz) dark chocolate
4 eggs
450g (15.87 Oz) sugar
150g (5.29 Oz) baking cocoa
200g (7.05 Oz) salted roasted peanuts

1. Preheat the oven 180°C (350°F). Grease the square springform pan (24 x 24 cm; alternatively, round, 26 cm Ø) and dust with flour. Break the chocolate into pieces. Melt with 8.8 Oz butter in a saucepan over low heat, stirring often.

2. Beat eggs and 8.81 Oz sugar with the whisk of the mixer for about 5 minutes until creamy. Mix the hot chocolate butter into the egg mixture in a thin stream. Sift 7.05 0z flour and 1.76 Oz cocoa on top and fold in. Mix in the peanuts. Pour the dough into the mould, smooth it out and bake for about 25 minutes (see tip).

3. Take the cake out of the oven and let it cool down. In the meantime, bring 1/4 l water, 7.05 Oz sugar and a pinch of salt to the boil for the chocolate sauce. Stir in 3.52 Oz cocoa with a whisk. Simmer for approx. 3 minutes while stirring. Pull from the stove and let cool down.

4. Cut the brownie into 4 cm cubes and serve with the chocolate sauce.

5. In the USA, the brownie layer is baked slightly "soggy". If you prefer your chocolate cake in the classic way, you should leave it in the oven for at least 10 minutes longer.

Blueberry Sundae

Ingredients for 4 people / 30 min (+ 720 min waiting time)

3 ripe bananas
1 organic lemon
100g (3.5 Oz) frozen blueberries
5 tbsp maple syrup
100g (3.5 Oz) Greek yogurt
3 tbsp cocoa nibs
50g (1.76 Oz) walnut kernels
1 large freezer bag

1. Peel 2 bananas the day before, cut into slices, place in a freezer bag and freeze.

2. Wash the lemon with hot water, dry it, thinly rub the peel, halve the fruit and squeeze out. For the sauce, briefly heat the blueberries in a saucepan, stir in 2 tablespoons of maple syrup and lemon zest. Finely puree the blueberry mix, strain through a sieve as desired and allow to cool.

3. Puree the frozen banana pieces with yogurt, lemon juice, 3 tablespoons of maple syrup, 2 tablespoons of cocoa nibs and 1.05 Oz of walnuts in a blender until creamy. Stir in the blueberry sauce.

4. Peel and slice the rest of the banana, roughly chop the rest of the nuts. Pour nice cream into glasses. Serve with banana slices, remaining cocoa nibs and nuts.

American Buttermilk Pancakes

2 eggs
50g (1.76 Oz) very soft butter
250ml (8.5 Fl Oz) buttermilk
180g (6.2 Oz) flour
1/2 tsp baking soda
1/2 tsp baking powder
1/2 tsp salt
1 tbsp sugar

1. Beat eggs, butter and buttermilk. Mix the flour, baking soda, baking powder, salt and sugar in an extra bowl, add to the egg mixture and stir.

2. Let the dough rest for a few minutes. Put the fat in a low to medium heated pan, spoon in the batter and bake the pancakes

3. Layer the pancakes and serve with maple syrup and / or jam.

Vegan Recipes

Crash Hot Potatoes

Ingredients for 4 people / 20 minutes

8 jacket potatoes
5 tbsp olive oil
2 garlic cloves
2 tbsp lemon juice
1 tsp sea-salt
1/2 tsp chili flakes
4 stem thyme
2 sprigs of rosemary

1. Preheat the oven 220°C (425°F). Lightly press 8 jacket potatoes inside the shell with a pounder (alternatively a spatula). Place on an oiled baking sheet.

2. For the seasoning oil, blend 5 tablespoons of olive oil with the garlic cloves, lemon juice, sea salt and chili flakes. Wash the thyme and rosemary, shake dry and cut into portions, add to the oil. Drizzle the spice oil over the potatoes.

3. Bake the potatoes within the hot oven for about 10 minutes.

Tofu Curry

Ingredients for 4 people / 25 min

500g (17.63 Oz) small carrots
300g (10.58 Oz) broccoli
1 shallot
200g (7.05 Oz) tofu
2 tbsp oil
50g (1.76 Oz) red curry paste
1 can (380g / 13.52 Fl Oz each) coconut milk
150g (5.29) frozen sugar snap peas
1 coriander
Salt

1. Peel and wash the carrots and cut in half of or sector lengthways depending on the size. Clean and wash broccolini. Peel the shallot and cut into skinny strips. Dice the tofu.

2. Fry the tofu in the hot oil, dispose of. Sauté shallot and carrots within the frying fat. Sweat the curry paste briefly. Deglaze with coconut milk and 200ml (6.76 Fl Oz) water, bring to the boil. Simmer for 8-10 mins.

3. Add the broccoli and frozen sugar snap peas and cook dinner for three–4 minutes. Add the tofu again and warmth in short. Wash the coriander, shake dry, pull off the leaves. Season the curry with salt and sprinkle with coriander. In addition: basmati rice.

Couscous Salad

Ingredients for 4 people / 40 minutes

9 tbsp oil
Salt
250g (8.81 Oz) couscous
60g (2.11 Oz) pine nuts
2 Carrots
1 onion
2 tbsp sugar
Pepper
1 large bunch of parsley
350g (12.34 Oz) strawberries
1 avocado
2 lemons (of which 1 organic)

1. For the couscous, boil 13.52 Fl oz water, 2 tablespoons oil and 1 teaspoon salt in a saucepan. Sprinkle with couscous. Remove the pot from the range. Cover the couscous and permit it to soak for about five minutes.

2. Toast the pine nuts in a pan until golden brown, take away. Peel and wash the carrots and cut into small cubes. Peel the onion and chop finely. Heat 1 tablespoon of oil in a pan. Sauté the carrots in it for two to –3 minutes. Add the onion and cook dinner for some other 2 mins. Sprinkle 2 tablespoons of sugar on pinnacle and caramelize lightly. Remove from heat, season with salt and pepper.

3. Wash the parsley and shake dry. Pluck leaves and finely chop. Wash, easy and chop the strawberries. Halve the avocado, put off the stone. Remove the pulp from the pores and skin and cut into small portions. Wash natural lemon with warm water and rub dry. Rub the peel finely. Squeeze each lemon.

4. In a big bowl, whisk collectively lemon juice and zest, salt and pepper. Beat in 6 tbsp oil. Mix the carrots, parsley, strawberries, avocado and vinaigrette. Fluff the couscous with a fork and blend incautiously. Season the salad with salt and pepper and let it steep briefly.

"Pulled Jack" BBQ burger

Ingredients for 4 people / 45 min

1 clove of garlic
2 tbsp tomato paste
3 tbsp olive oil
1 tsp, levelled Pimento de la Vera (smoked paprika powder)
Salt + pepper
1 pack (200g / 7.05 Oz each) young jackfruit pieces
250g (8.81 Oz) red cabbage
4 tbsp apple cider vinegar
2 tbsp rice syrup
1 Mini lettuce cucumber
4 stems parsley
50g (1.76 Oz) roasted peppers (pickled)
2 onions
4 chia protein buns
2 tbsp vegan mayonnaise
2 tbsp cashew nuts for sprinkling

1. For the marinade, peel and finely chop the garlic. Mix with tomato paste, 4 tbsp water, 2 tbsp oil, paprika, a touch of salt and pepper. Mix with the jackfruit portions and gently mash the portions. Let it steep for 15–30 minutes.

2. In the intervening time, wash the red cabbage and reduce into first-rate strips until the stalk. Knead with salt, pepper, vinegar and rice syrup, let it steep. Wash the cucumber and reduce lengthways into satisfactory slices. Wash the parsley, shake dry and pluck the leaves off. Drain the roasted peppers and cut into best strips

3. Peel the onions and cut into pleasant strips. Heat 1 tablespoon of oil in a pan, fry the onions in it for approximately 2 minutes. Add the marinated jackfruit and retain frying over high warmness for approximately four minutes, turning.

4. Cut the rolls open and brush with mayonnaise. Top with the coleslaw, cucumber slices, roasted peppers, parsley and jackfruit. Finely chop the cashews and sprinkle over them. Put the bread roll lid on.

Palak Tofu

Ingredients for 2 people / 40 minutes

2 onions
2 garlic cloves
1 piece ginger
1 red chili pepper
250g (1/2 lb) organic tofu
2 tbsp oil
1/4 tsp ground cloves
1 tsp ground cumin
1 tsp ground coriander
1 tsp turmeric
500g (1lb) frozen spinach leaves
salt
1 tsp garam masala

1. Peel the onions, garlic and ginger. Finely dice the onions and garlic, grate the ginger. Cut the chilli lengthways, get rid of the seeds, wash and cut into skinny rings. Cut the tofu into cubes.

2. Heat oil in a pan. Fry the tofu in it for 2-3 mins on each side cast off. Fry the onions, garlic, ginger, chili, cloves, cumin, coriander and turmeric within the hot frying fats whilst stirring until it smells of the spices.

3. Add the frozen spinach and 100ml (3.38 Fl Oz) water and stir in. Cover and prepare dinner over low warmth for about 15 minutes. Season to taste with salt. Add the tofu to the spinach and warmth in brief. Stir within the garam masala.

4. Serving. Mango lassi, chapati (thin Indian flatbread) or basmati rice also taste right.

Roasted Vegetable salad

Ingredients for 8 people / 60 minutes

100g (2lb) potatoes
Salt pepper
8 tbsp high quality olive oil
2 red onions
2 yellow peppers
500g (1lb) Oz broccoli
6 tbsp white wine vinegar
1 tbsp Dijon mustard
1 tbsp liquid honey
3–4 stem flat leaf parsley

1. Preheat the oven 200°C (400°F). Peel and wash the potatoes and cut into cubes (approx. 2 x 2 cm). Season with salt and drizzle with 2 tablespoons of oil. Cook in a pan (deep baking tray; 32 x 39 cm) in the warm oven for about 45 minutes.

2. From time to time to show.

3. In the interim, peel the onions and cut into wedges. Clean, wash and dice the peppers. Cut the broccoli into florets from the stalk and wash. After about 25 minutes of cooking, add the peppers and onions to the potatoes.

4. Add the broccoli florets for the remaining 10 mins.

5. For the vinaigrette, whisk collectively vinegar, salt, pepper, mustard and honey. Beat in 6 tbsp oil. Wash the parsley, shake dry, pluck the leaves off and chop finely.

6. Take the vegetables out of the oven and blend with the vinaigrette. Let settle down. Mix in the parsley. Season the salad again to taste and serve.

Quinoa Salad

Ingredients for 4 people / 30 minutes

250g (8.81 Oz) quinoa
1/4 cucumber
150g (5.25 Oz) Cherry tomatoes
1 Red onion
1/4 bunch dill
1 tsp mustard
Sugar
1 tsp Apple Cider Vinegar
Juice of 1 lemon
1 tbsp olive oil
Salt
Pepper
1 can (210g / 7.16 Fl Oz) Corn
Sprouts and cress

1. Bring quinoa to a boil with 240ml (8.11 Fl Oz) water. Let it simmer until the water has completely evaporated. Let the quinoa cool down. Peel and finely cube the cucumber. Wash, easy and halve tomatoes. Peel the onion and chop finely.

2. Wash dill, shake dry and finely chop. Mix the mustard, a pinch of sugar, vinegar and lemon juice, beat inside the oil. Season with salt and pepper. Stir in the dill. Drain the corn. Mix the cucumber, tomatoes, onion and corn with the quinoa.

3. Mix the dressing into the salad. Sprinkle with sprouts and cress.

Soul Comfort Recipes

Lentil Falafel

Ingredients For 2 Servings / 30 minutes

1 tbsp butter
125g (4.41 oz) Lentils, red
220ml (8.45 Fl oz) water
Vegetable stock cubes
Onion
Egg
2 Garlic cloves)
3 tbsp Parsley, fresh (optional)
1 tbsp Coriander, fresh (optional)
2 tbsp Flour
1 teaspoon Paprika powder
1 teaspoon Ground cumin

1. Swirl the lentils in the butter and sauté briefly. Add 1/4 litre (quart) of water and the vegetable stock cube and cook covered for about 20 minutes over medium heat.

2. In the meantime, chop the onion, parsley and coriander.

3. If the lentils have not disintegrated after 20 minutes, puree them briefly. Let the mixture cool down briefly and add all the other ingredients. Shape the mixture into small cakes.

4. Heat the oil in a pan, depending on your taste, and fry the falafel for about 2 minutes on each side.

5. Tastes great with fried vegetables and a tahini dip or with a salad, e.g., tabbouleh.

Sweet Potato Fries

Ingredients For 2 Servings / 30 minutes

3 Sweet potato
Salt
Oil

1. Peel the sweet potatoes and cut into French fries. Place the potatoes on a baking sheet lined with baking paper, drizzle with a little oil and bake at 200°C (400°F) for about 20 minutes. Be careful not to burn them, sweet potatoes cook faster in the oven than normal potatoes.

2. The French fries taste very good even without spices, but they only really develop their great taste when they are sprinkled with a pinch of salt after baking.

3. The potatoes can also be sprinkled with salt, pepper, cumin, cayenne pepper or similar before baking.

Carrot-Ginger–Soup

Ingredients for 4 servings / 20 minutes

60g (2.11 oz) Ginger, fresher
400g (14.19 oz) Carrot
50g (1.76 oz) butter
1 tbsp sugar
600ml (20.28 Fl oz) Vegetable broth
150ml (5.07 Fl oz) Coconut milk
Salt and pepper

1. Peel the ginger and dice it very finely so that no fibres can be felt later after pureeing. Peel the carrots and cut into thin slices.

2. Sweat the carrots and ginger in butter, then sprinkle the sugar over them and let them caramelize slightly. Deglaze with the stock and coconut milk and bring to the boil. Let the soup simmer over medium heat for about 20 minutes, then puree finely with a hand blender. Season to taste with salt and pepper.

3. The slight spiciness of the ginger offers a special taste experience. Toast or baguette can be served with the soup.

Stuffed Peppers

Ingredients for 4 servings / 40 minutes

10 Pointed peppers, yellow, possibly more depending on the size
500g (1lb) Minced meat pork or beef
Onion
1 toe garlic
Salt and pepper, black from the mill
Paprika powder
100g (3.52 oz) Rice, cooked
Egg
1 small Can Tomato paste
500 ml (17 Fl oz) Vegetable broth
Sugar
1 tbsp butter
1 tbsp Flour

1. Make a minced meat dough from minced meat, rice, egg, onion and garlic and season with the spices. Pour into the peppers and use the rest to form meatballs.

2. Melt the butter in a saucepan, add the flour and roast a little. Deglaze with the vegetable stock, add the tomato paste and bring to the boil. Season to taste with salt, pepper and a little sugar. Put the filled peppers and the balls in the sauce and stew either on the stove or in the oven for 30-40 minutes.

3. There is also rice.

4. Alternatively, you can use tomato puree instead of the tomato paste. Then use a little less broth.

5. The quantities are of course a bit vague, my Uri always cooked "by feeling". I tried to follow the recipe as closely as possible

Chicken Curry with Chickpeas and Mango

Ingredients For 4 Servings / 30 minutes

500g (17.63 oz) Chicken breast
Onion
Mango
1 tbsp honey
2 tbsp Curry powder
1 teaspoon Ginger, freshly grated
1 pinch Lemon zest kaffir lemon leaves
1 stem Coriander green
400ml (13.5 Fl oz) chicken broth
400ml (13.5 Fl oz) Coconut milk
1 can Chickpeas
Oil
Basmati rice

For decoration:

sour cream
Coriander green

1. Cut the poultry breast into approx. 2 cm cubes. Peel the onion, cut in half and finely dice. Peel the mango, remove the stone and cut the pulp into approx. 2 cm cubes.

2. Fry the meat and onion together in a little oil in a large flat saucepan or pan until golden. Turn down the heat a little, add the curry, stir and let it sear a little. Add the mango, honey, ginger, drained chickpeas and kaffir lemon leaves or zest of the lemon. Top up with broth and coconut milk and reduce to a creamy consistency. Finally, cut some coriander into small pieces and add to the chicken curry.

3. Prepare the rice according to the instructions on the packet.

4. Serving: Place the rice in the middle of the plate, pour the chicken curry on top or next to it and garnish with a spoonful of sour cream and coriander leaves.

Autumn Salad with Fried Pumpkin, Caramelized Pear, Blue Cheese and Walnuts

Ingredients For 4 Servings / 35 minutes

Enough Salad for 4 people (e.g., lamb's lettuce, oak leaf, ...)
Pear, ripe
1 teaspoon sugar
150g (5.3 oz Pumpkin), Hokkaido (with edible skin)
1 tbsp butter
nutmeg
10 Walnuts
300g (10.58 oz) Blue cheese (Roquefort, Stilton or Gorgonzola)
3 tbsp Vinegar, (white wine vinegar)
7 tbsp Oil, (grapeseed oil)
1 tbsp Pumpkin seed oil
salt and pepper
sugar

1. Wash and clean the lettuce.

2. Peel and quarter the pear, remove the core and cut diagonally into diamonds. Caramelize the sugar in a pan and briefly toss the pear in it.

3. Cut the pumpkin with the skin into pieces or wedges. Fry or cook them briefly in a pan with butter. Season with salt, nutmeg and pepper.

4. Roughly chop walnuts and toast them in a pan without oil.

5. In a bowl, whisk the vinegar and spices together with a whisk. Slowly add both types of oil.

For Serving:

Arrange the salad on a plate and marinate with the dressing.

Chop up the cheese and spread on top with the pear, pumpkin and nuts.

Hearty Lentil Stew with Vegetables and Sausages

Ingredients For 4 Servings / 1 hour

250g (8.81 oz) Lentils, dried, soak in water
Onion
2 large Carrot
2 large Potato
1 piece celery root
1 piece Bacon rind
2 tbsp Rapeseed oil
1 shot vinegar
1 tbsp mustard
1 l (quart) vegetable broth
4 Sausages, hearty and / or Kassel slices
salt and pepper
sugar
nutmeg
Parsley, finely chopped

1. Peel the onion and cut into fine cubes. Clean and dice the root vegetables. Fry everything together in a saucepan with oil and the bacon rind.

2. Depending on the type of lentils, soak them (follow the instructions on the packaging) and add to the vegetables with any remaining soaking water. Let the soaking water boil off. Then deglaze with vinegar and let it boil. Add the vegetable stock, potatoes cut into pieces and mustard. Let everything simmer for about 20-30 minutes.

3. Cut the sausages or smoked pork into bite-sized pieces, add them and let them infuse in the stew. Season with salt, pepper, nutmeg and sugar and add finely chopped parsley.

Ratatouille

Ingredients For 4 Servings / 30 minutes

2 tbsp Tomato paste
100 ml (3.38 Fl oz) water
2 Bell pepper
Aubergine (Eggplant)
Courgette (Zucchini)
Onion, red
1 toe garlic
rosemary
salt and pepper

1. Cut the zucchini, onion, garlic and bell pepper into cubes. If you like, you can peel the peppers. To do this, quarter and core the peppers, then place in the oven at 200°C (400°F) for 15 minutes and peel off the skin. Finally, dice the aubergine as it will brown quickly.

2. Fry the vegetables one by one. First fry the zucchini and take them out of the pan. Then fry the peppers and place in the same bowl as the zucchini. Finally fry the eggplant with the rosemary and add to the vegetables. Now fry the red onion briefly. Add the tomato paste to the onions with a small splash of water. Now add the previously fried vegetables. Warm everything up briefly and season with salt and pepper.

Onion Soup

Ingredients For 4 Servings / 45 minutes

1 kg (2.2 lb) Vegetable onion
5 tbsp Oil, neutral
2 tbsp Flour
Salt and pepper, black, freshly ground
2 Tea spoons sugar
1 litre (quart) vegetable broth, strong
300 ml (10.65 Fl oz) white wine, drier
1.76 oz butter
5 slice Baguette or toast bread
8 tbsp Gruyere, grated
4 pinches Paprika powder, noble sweet

1. Peel the onions and cut into fine rings - that's the original. The soup is sometimes very difficult to spoon, so it makes sense to halve or quarter the onions and then cut or slice them into fine rings.

2. Heat the oil in a large saucepan and fry the onions until the onion juice has leaked out. Dust the onions with the flour, season with sugar, salt and pepper and mix thoroughly. Gradually pour in the wine and then the broth and simmer for 15 minutes with the lid slightly open.

3. Meanwhile, heat the butter in a pan and fry the bread slices until crispy brown. Here, too, if you want it to be easier to eat, you should cut the baguette a little smaller, but in the original, whole slices are on it. These swim better, of course.

4. Pour the onion soup into bowls, place the baguette slices on top of the onion soup, sprinkle with cheese and paprika. Bake the soup in the top of the oven or under the grill until golden brown and serve immediately.

Risotto with Lemon, Mint and Pepper

Ingredients For 4 Servings / 30 to 60 min

180g (6.34 oz) Riso Arborio Gran Gallo
shallots
extra virgin olive oil
40g (1.41 oz) parmesan (grated)
40g (1.41 oz) butter
360g (12.84 Fl oz) vegetable soup (clear, approx.)
mint leaves
1/2 lemon (organic)
a pair of peppercorns (crushed)

1. For the risotto with lemon, mint and pepper, first peel the lemon peel with a peeler and cut into very thin strips. Cut shallots into thin strips and sauté in a saucepan with olive oil and butter until translucent.

2. Add the rice. Only when the rice is translucent and warm, add the hot vegetable soup, creator by creator, stirring constantly. Do not add the soup until the rice has absorbed the liquid.

3. When the rice is done but still bite, let it rest for a few minutes, then stir in the butter and parmesan.

4. Place the risotto on the plates using a serving ring. Garnish with lemon zest, mint and pepper.

5. The risotto with lemon, mint and pepper Serve hot.

Tuna Spaghetti

Ingredients For 2 Servings / 15 to 30 min

250g (8.81 oz) spaghetti
1 onion
1 clove of garlic
pickles
1 handful of capers
1 handful of olives (green)
1 can of tuna (natural, without oil)
1/2 bunch of chives
120g (4.22 Fl oz) whipped cream (more if desired)
salt
Pepper (from the mill)
1/2 lemon (juice and zest)

1. Cook the spaghetti in salted water according to the instructions on the package until al dente.

2. Peel onion and garlic and chop finely. Drain the pickles and cut into small cubes. Halve the capers. Roughly chop the olives. Drain the tuna. Wash and finely chop the chives.

3. Heat the olive oil in a pan and sweat the onion cubes in it. Add the garlic. Then add the tuna, olives, capers and cucumber. Fry briefly and then mix with the whipped cream. Season to taste with salt, pepper and lemon juice and zest.

4. Add the spaghetti and mix well.

5. Sprinkle the tuna spaghetti with chives.

6. If you want, you can serve freshly grated Parmesan with the tuna spaghetti.

Cannelloni Bolognese

Ingredients For 2 Servings / 60 min

Butter (for the mould)
250g (8.81 oz) cannelloni
50g (1.76 oz) parmesan (freshly grated, for sprinkling)

For the Bolognese sauce:

tomatoes
1 can Polpo (peeled, finely chopped tomatoes, approx. 400 g / 14oz)
1 tbsp tomato paste (from the tube)
onions
1 clove of garlic
3 tbsp olive oil
400g (14 oz) minced meat pork or beef
sea-salt
Pepper (from the mill)
1/2 bunch of basil

For the Bechamel sauce:

50g (1.7 oz) butter
30g (1.1 oz) of flour
500g (16.9 Fl oz) milk (a little more if required)
50g (1.7 oz) parmesan (finely grated)

1. First peel the onion and chop it as finely as possible. Peel the garlic clove and press it through a garlic press.

2. Blanch the tomatoes in hot water, rinse in cold water and peel, then dice finely.

3. Wash, pluck and chop the basil.

4. For the Bolognese sauce, heat the oil in a pan. Sweat the onion and garlic in it until translucent, add the tomato paste and minced meat and roast until crumbly. Add the polpa and diced tomatoes and let the sauce simmer for a few minutes.

5. In the meantime, melt the butter in a saucepan for the bechamel sauce. Sprinkle in flour and toast briefly over medium heat (it shouldn't brown).

6. Pour half of the milk into the flour and butter mixture and stir thoroughly with a whisk. Let thicken briefly, then stir in the rest of the milk and parmesan, let the sauce thicken again and finally season with salt and a little nutmeg.

7. Stir the basil into the Bolognese sauce and season with salt and pepper. Allow to cool slightly. Preheat the oven to 180°C (350°F). Grease a baking dish.

8. Fill the cannelloni with the sauce using a dressing sack (or a teaspoon). Then place them close together in the prepared baking dish, pour the bechamel sauce over them and sprinkle with parmesan.

9. Bake in the preheated oven for about 45 minutes.

Classic Layered Salad Cake

Ingredients For 2 Servings / 30 to 60 min

For the salad:

sheets of lettuce
150g (5.3 oz) corn
1/4 pineapple
1/2 stick leek
1/3 stick celery
1 apple
eggs
slices of ham
slice cheese (grated)
1 bunch of wild garlic (or other herbs)

For the dressing:

75g (2.6 oz) mayonnaise
50g (1.7 oz) sour cream
50g (1.7 oz) yogurt

1/2 lemon (juice)
1/2 orange (juice)
salt
pepper

To decorate:

1 handful of salad (mixed)
pieces of radishes
1 handful of leeks
flowers (edible)
Apple cubes (as you like)

1. Wash the iceberg lettuce, cut off about 6 leaves, pluck into a round shape and drain thoroughly.

2. Peel the pineapple and dice it. Wash the apple, celery and leek and cut into small pieces. Now wash the radishes and cut them into thin slices.

3. Turn the corn out of the can and let it dry well.

4. Boil the eggs hard, peel them and cut them into slices.

5. Now put a cake ring on a plate and, starting with the salad, layer the cake as follows: ham, leek, corn, sauce, wild garlic, eggs, pineapple, apples, dressing and cheese.

6. Let the cake cool in the refrigerator for a few minutes between layers.

7. Before decorating, carefully remove the cake ring and only then start decorating. Top the salad cake with the sliced celery, leek and some lettuce leaves. Put the sliced radishes and edible flowers on top and finish off the nest with small apple cubes.

Chocolate Dumplings

Ingredients For 4 Servings / 15 to 30 min

10 pieces of chocolate
50g (1.76 oz) butter
1 handful of breadcrumbs
Icing sugar (for sprinkling)

For the dough:

250g (8.81 oz) curd cheese
1 egg
125g (4.41 oz) flour
60g (2.11 oz) butter
some salt

1. First mix the curd cheese, egg, flour, butter and salt and knead into a dough.

2. Divide the dough into 10 equal pieces and press each flat. Place a piece of chocolate in the middle and cover it completely with the potting mixture.

3. Bring the water to a boil and then turn it back a little so that it simmers gently.

4. Carefully insert the dumplings and let them steep for about 10 minutes. They are done when they swim to the surface.

5. For the crumbs, melt the butter in a pan. Mix the breadcrumbs with the cinnamon and toast them in the butter.

6. Roll the chocolate dumplings in the breadcrumbs and serve sprinkled with icing sugar.

Banana Milk

Ingredients For 2 Servings / 5 to 15 min

2 bananas
1 packet of vanilla sugar
400ml (13.5 Fl oz) of milk
Lemon juice

1. First peel the bananas and mix them with vanilla sugar, lemon juice and milk.

2. Mix in a few ice cubes if necessary.

3. Serve the banana milk immediately.

4. Depending on how sweet and thick the banana milk should be, the amount of sugar or milk can be varied as desired.

Feel free to contact me if you have any questions or suggestions:

bellesourcebooks@gmail.com

Join our "The Quokka Gourmet" email list to receive a **free recipe book** and stay informed about future books:

→ bit.ly/3DMTSCm ←

My books can't be successful without **YOUR help.** It would mean the world to me if you could **leave a review on Amazon.**

Thank you

Imperial / Metric Conversion chart

U.S. Volume Measure	Metric Equivalent
$1/8$ teaspoon	0.5 millilitre
$1/4$ teaspoon	1 millilitre
$1/2$ teaspoon	2 millilitres
1 teaspoon	5 millilitres
$1/2$ tablespoon	7 millilitres
1 tablespoon (3 teaspoons)	15 millilitres
2 tablespoons (1 fluid ounce)	30 millilitres
$1/4$ cup (4 tablespoons)	60 millilitres
$1/3$ cup	90 millilitres
$1/2$ cup (4 fluid ounces)	125 millilitres
$2/3$ cup	160 millilitres
$3/4$ cup (6 fluid ounces)	180 millilitres
1 cup (16 tablespoons)	250 millilitres
1 pint (2 cups)	500 millilitres
1 quart (4 cups)	1 litre (about)

U.S. Weight Measure	Metric Equivalent
$1/2$ ounce	15 grams
1 ounce	30 grams
2 ounces	60 grams
3 ounces	85 grams
$1/4$ pound (4 ounces)	115 grams
$1/2$ pound (8 ounces)	225 grams
3/4 pound (12 ounces)	340 grams
1 pound (16 ounces)	454 grams

Imprint / Impressum

Copyright © 2022 Jean Bellesource
All rights reserved

„Jean Bellesource" wird vertreten durch
Tobias Schöneborn
Augustin-Wibbelt-Str. 4
46242 Bottrop
thequokkagourmet@gmail.com
ISBN: 9798794330366
Imprint: Independently published

Text: Andre Anna
Images: Licensed by Envato Elements, Pexels, IStock

Liability for links
Our book contains links to external websites of third parties, on whose contents we have no influence. Therefore, we cannot assume any liability for these external contents. The respective provider or operator of the sites is always responsible for the content of the linked sites. The linked pages were checked for possible legal violations at the time of linking. Illegal contents were not recognizable at the time of linking. However, a permanent control of the contents of the linked pages is not reasonable without concrete evidence of a violation of the law. If we become aware of any infringements, we will remove such links immediately.

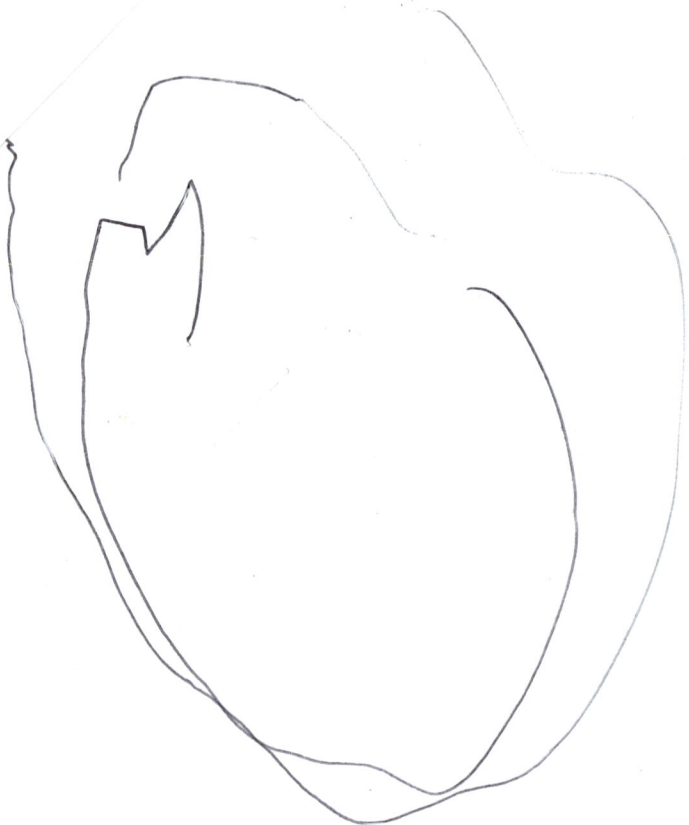

Printed in Great Britain
by Amazon